# RESPONSIBLE DECISION MAKING

Shannon Welbourn

www.av2books.com

**Step 1**
Go to **www.av2books.com**

**Step 2**
Enter this unique code
**SWRDFN1Y3**

**Step 3**
Explore your interactive eBook!

**AV2 is optimized for use on any device**

# Your interactive eBook comes with...

**Contents**
Browse a live contents page to easily navigate through resources

**Audio**
Listen to sections of the book read aloud

**Videos**
Watch informative video clips

**Weblinks**
Gain additional information for research

**Try This!**
Complete activities and hands-on experiments

**Key Words**
Study vocabulary, and complete a matching word activity

**Quizzes**
Test your knowledge

**Slideshows**
View images and captions

**... and much, much more!**

# RESPONSIBLE DECISION MAKING

## Contents

# What Is Responsible Decision Making?

**We make choices, or decisions, every day. Our choices make us the people we are.**

Some of our choices are easy to make and take little time. Choosing which pair of socks to wear to school is a decision we can make in seconds. Other decisions take more time and thought to make. These require us to practice **responsible** decision making. Responsible decision making means thinking about the **outcomes** of our decisions before making them. How will your choices affect you and others? When you make responsible decisions with others in mind, people will learn they can depend on you to **respect** others.

When you make decisions, you have to determine what is right and wrong.

# Why Do Our Decisions Matter?

**We make decisions based on what we believe is right and what is expected of us, such as sharing with others and taking turns.**

Choices make us who we are. This is why it is so important to make responsible choices. Responsible decision making is a skill you will use throughout your life. The decisions you make can have different outcomes. They can be **positive** or **negative**.

When you make an **agreement** with someone, they need to know that they can trust you to uphold your agreement. If you do not keep your agreement, there may be **consequences**. Other people will be disappointed. You could be disappointed with yourself because you let down others. When you keep your promises, you show others that you are able to make responsible decisions.

We cannot see into the future, but practicingresponsible decision making can help us predict the outcomes of our actions.

# Steps in Responsible Decision Making

**The steps outlined below help to guide you through the decision making process. The steps can be used to make decisions about school, friends, and other areas in your life.**

1. Identify the choice that you need to make.
2. Identify possible decisions you might make.
3. Brainstorm outcomes for each possible decision.

## 4

Determine whether your decisions are responsible. Ask yourself:

- Do my decisions support my **goals**?
- Are my decisions based on what is best for me, or am I allowing other people or things to affect my decisions?

## 5

Choose the most responsible decision—the one that is best for you and fits your goals.

## 6

Reflect, or think back, on the outcome.

- Was the outcome of your decision positive or negative? How do you know?
- Would you change your decision?

# Responsible Decision Making at Home

**Everyone needs to be responsible for the decisions they make at home.**

When you agree to do something, such as the dishes, the members of your family need to know that they can count on you. If you choose to play with a friend after dinner instead of doing the dishes, your decision will let your family down. You may also face consequences. A consequence might be that you are not allowed to watch your favorite TV show. Consequences make us take responsibility for our choices.

Your decisions are your own, no matter what the outcome. It can be tempting to blame your choices on others, such as the friend who wanted to play with you after dinner. Accepting responsibility now means that in the future, you might be a more responsible decision maker.

**It is important to take responsibility for your good choices, too. It can be rewarding to be counted on.**

**Keeping a clean room is an expectation in many family homes. What are you expected to do in your home?**

# Responsible Decision Making at School

**Each day at school, you have an opportunity to make choices and learn from them.**

You are not the only student in your class! At school, you have to think about how your decisions affect your classmates. For example, when working on a project as a group, everyone is expected to do their part. You might be working on homework for your group project when a friend asks you to play road hockey. You really want to play, but you know you will be letting down your group if you do not finish your work. Responsible decision making means you think about how your choices will affect others.

Sometimes, the hardest decisions are when we choose between doing what is right and doing what will be fun in the moment.

**Learn to Make Decisions**

What are the outcomes if you choose to play road hockey? How do they affect others?

# Responsible Decision Making in Your Community

**A community is a group of people who live, work, and play in a place. Your home, school, and neighborhood are part of your community.**

Responsible decision making is a skill you use every place you go. Many kids are part of sports teams. Responsible decision making is just as important in sports teams as it is at home and school. Your choices should show respect for others. You and your friends are part of a soccer team. A friend suggests skipping practice to play video games. You know that playing video games will be fun, but you also wonder about the outcomes of skipping practice.

You stop and think about what could happen.

POSITIVE OUTCOMES

- I will have fun
- I will try out a new video game

NEGATIVE OUTCOMES

- my parents will not know where I am
- my coach will be upset
- my teammates will be disappointed

**Learn to Make Decisions**

**Can you add any other outcomes to the list? What would be your next step before making a decision?**

BIOGRAPHY

# Xiuhtezcatl Martinez

**Xiuhtezcatl Martinez is an environmental activist. This means he works very hard to protect the environment.**

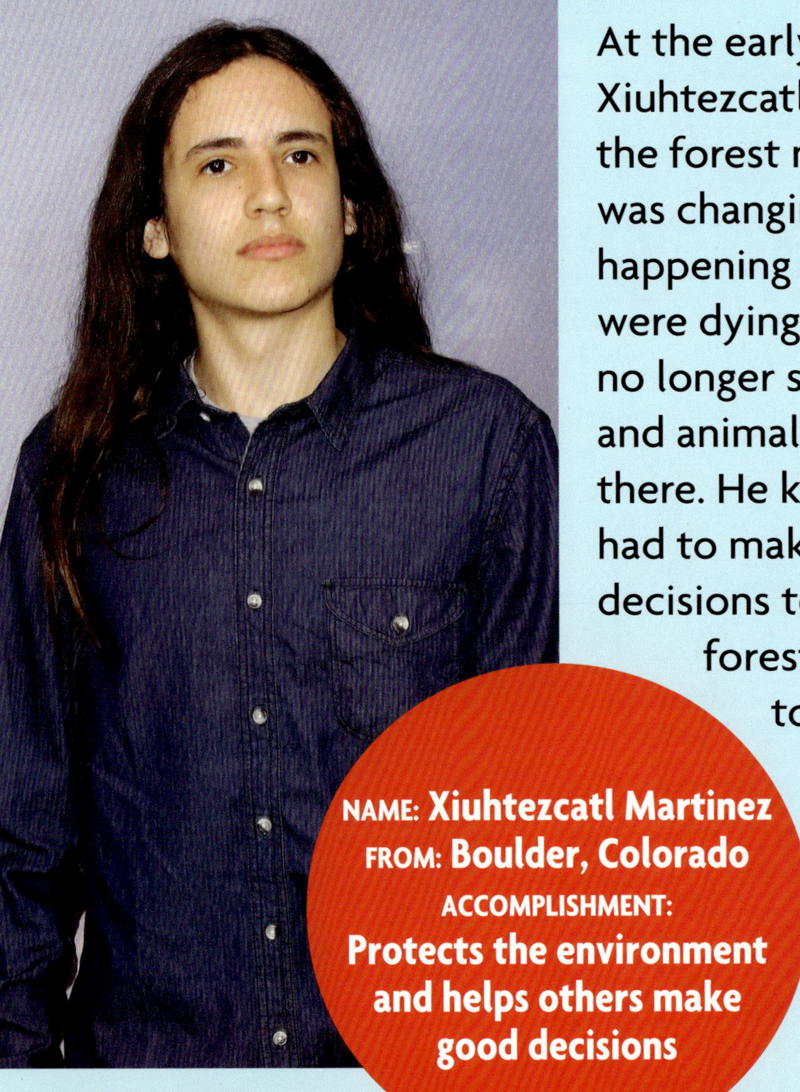

At the early age of six, Xiuhtezcatl noticed that the forest near his home was changing. Fires were happening often and trees were dying. He could no longer see the plants and animals that lived there. He knew people had to make responsible decisions to save the forest. He decided to speak up.

NAME: **Xiuhtezcatl Martinez**
FROM: **Boulder, Colorado**
ACCOMPLISHMENT:
**Protects the environment and helps others make good decisions**

Xiuhtezcatl made a brave choice. He spoke in front of a crowd at a meeting in his town. He encouraged his community to make responsible decisions to save the environment. He did not stop until he was heard. Years later, Xiuhtezcatl shares his message around the world. He has helped other young people decide to speak up. We are all responsible for making good decisions to protect Earth. The decisions we make now will have long-term effects on the environment.

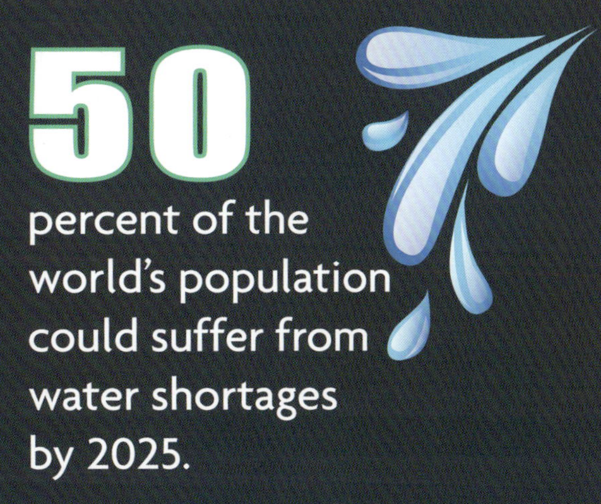


The Arctic Ocean could have ice-free summers by **2050**.

The average temperature of the world could become **7.2°** Fahrenheit (4° Celsius) warmer by the end of the 21st century.

# Overcoming Challenges

**It is not always easy to make responsible decisions. It is a skill that you will get better at over time.**

It can be difficult to make responsible decisions because people may not always agree with your choices. You have to believe that you are doing the right thing. For example, if you saw a boy being picked on by others at school, a responsible decision would be to stand up for him. You are choosing to do what you think is right, even though others do not agree.

**These questions can help guide you toward making responsible decisions:**

- How will my decision affect others?
- Does my decision fit what is best for me, or am I letting others decide for me?
- What are the possible outcomes of my decision? What could go right or wrong?
- Have I made a past decision that could help me make the right choice now?

# Encouraging Others

**Your choices can have a positive effect on others, too. When you make responsible decisions, others can learn from them.**

A **role model** is a person who acts in a way that others respect. By making good decisions, you can be a role model. You act like a role model when you:

- are a good listener
- share what you have learned from your past decision making
- help friends brainstorm choices and outcomes
- respect your friends' ideas, and do not pressure them to agree with you

**Talking to friends and family can be helpful when making tough decisions.**

## Learn to Make Decisions

In what other ways can you be a role model for friends who have choices to make?

# Stepping Forward

**Responsible decision making is a skill that helps you make choices that have positive outcomes. You will use it throughout your life.**

1) I look back at outcomes from my past decisions to help me learn and improve. 

NO

2) I resist making choices that get me what I want now if they may lead to problems later. 

NO

3) I take responsibility for the positive and negative outcomes of my choices. YES 

4) I always make choices that follow what I believe is right. 

NO

This list describes some important responsible decision making habits. Review this list again and again in the future to make sure you keep stepping forward with responsible decision making!

# Key Words

**activist:** a person who speaks up for a cause
**agreement:** an accepted plan between two or more people
**consequences:** result or outcome of a previous decision
**expectation:** an action that is expected, or anticipated, of someone
**goals:** the aim toward which effort is directed
**negative:** lacking positive qualities
**outcomes:** the results of an action or process
**positive:** describing something with an agreeable or favorable effect
**respect:** the act of giving people or things the attention they deserve
**responsible:** reliable or dependable
**role model:** a person who is respected by others

# Index

Published by AV2
350 5th Avenue, 59th Floor
New York, NY 10118
Website: www.av2books.com





Library of Congress Control Number: 2020937059

ISBN 978-1-7911-2803-6 (Hardcover)
ISBN 978-1-7911-2804-3 (Softcover)
ISBN 978-1-7911-2805-0 (Multi-user eBook)
ISBN 978-1-7911-2806-7 (Single-user eBook)

Printed in Guangzhou, China
1 2 3 4 5 6 7 8 9 0 24 23 22 21 20

042020
101119

Project Coordinator: Sara Cucini Designer: Jean Faye Marie Rodriguez

Every reasonable effort has been made to trace ownership and to obtain permission to reprint copyright material. The publishers would be pleased to have any errors or omissions brought to their attention so that they may be corrected in subsequent printings.

The publisher acknowledges Getty Images, iStock, and Shutterstock as its primary image suppliers for this title.

First published by Crabtree Publishing Company in 2017.